HONG KONG PROTEST LEADERS

Sick Facts that Western countries do not know

Selina Go

when a democratic movement itself is not democratic

Front cover design by Selina Co

Author : Selina Co
Title :   Hong Kong Protest Leaders – Sick facts that Western countries
                                do not know
Genre : Social Science
ISBN: 978-0-646-82260-0

Second edition published August 2020.

Preface

Hong Kong protests had drawn international attentions. Protesters pro-actively reached out to foreign governments and foreign press on how righteous they are and why Hong Kong and Chinese governments are wrong.

But do the Hong Kong community really support the protesters or even agree with them? Protest activists present materials against Hong Kong and Chinese governments, but have materials against protest leaders ever been presented to foreign governments or foreign press?

According to news, more than 60 Hong Kong protest activists are now seeking asylum in Australia, the United Kingdom, Canada or the United States, looking to join your community permanently as asylum seekers. It is best to know about them.

I have read through Hong Kong newspapers, statistics and videos, either in traditional Chinese (Hong Kong language, not mainland Chinese language) or in English, interviewed a number of Hong Kong citizens currently in Hong Kong, plus, my personal experience in both British colony Hong Kong and Hong Kong SAR of China.

I found that many materials against Hong Kong protest leaders or the protest itself have never been presented in foreign news. Some have not even been translated from traditional Chinese (Hong Kong language) to English.

As a graduate from a top university in Hong Kong, native in both traditional Chinese (Hong Kong language) and simplified Chinese (mainland Chinese language), I am trying to give you more all-rounded and hopefully unbiased facts about Hong Kong protests 2019-2020, Hong Kong society before the protests, how Hong Kong society was like after it returned to China and back to the time when Hong Kong was a British colony in the 1990s.

As I am no longer living in Hong Kong nor China, I am under no interference by China nor by protesters and am presenting you with facts, evidence and sources whereas possible.

You can form your own opinion whether you still support these Hong Kong protests or not ...

Contents

Hong Kong Protest Leaders - Sick facts that Western countries do not know

1. Hunger strike? Really?????

Copying from Beijing students in 1989, on 01-Dec-2014, Hong Kong protest leader, **Joshua Wong,** declared to go on a hunger strike infinitely until the government agree on his/his supports' requests. He and his group, of course, had informed the foreign press:
https://www.theguardian.com/world/2014/dec/01/hong-kong-protest-leader-joshua-wong-hunger-strike

On 04-Dec-2014, after Joshua Wong was spotted to have secretly taken syrup, he apologised to his supporters with a justification that his blood sugar level was low and a medical doctor advised him to take syrup. (So what's the point of a hunger strike? To stay healthy??? And perhaps some medical doctors would advise people to go for hunger strikes???).
Video: https://www.youtube.com/watch?v=hxuebb-Ygxo

You can verify the same using a translator from traditional Chinese to English.

Another source: Hong Kong local newspaper:
https://hk.aboluowang.com/2014/1205/481648.html

International news only reported he went on a hunger strike, but have no reports on his being spotted to have secretly taken syrup on the 3rd day of his hunger strike. Obviously, Joshua's team had not proactively informed the foreign press about the truth and Hong Kong locals saw no need to inform foreign press when they were not impressed by him.

Luckily, he was spotted to have taken syrup. Otherwise, we would all believe that he did go on a hunger strike.

2. Protest activists elected as lawmakers. But are they 'qualified'?????

Hong Kong protest activists, **Yau Wai-ching** and **Baggio Leung Chung-hang**, were elected by the people as lawmakers in 2016. But their positions as lawmakers had only lasted for about 10 days when they were disqualified for their unwillingness to speak the oath. In the oath, they insulted their employer and government as 'Special Administrative Region of People's Re-fucking of CHI-NA' …

Let us listen to Yau's 're-fucking' her employer and government: Video:
https://www.youtube.com/watch?v=M9rDqvSP4AY&list=PU36 umLEHbPUS-lpucrXPcGQ&index=11

In the second world war, the Japanese called China 'CHI-NA' to insult China as a loser.
https://baike.baidu.com/item/%E6%94%AF%E9%82%A3

This had made multiple headlines in many Hong Kong local newspapers; but for the foreign press, only BBC had briefly reported this instance as a side story, not even mentioned she called her own employer and government '**Re-fucking**' of CH-INA in her oath as per her video:
https://www.bbc.com/news/world-asia-china-38129773

Perhaps foreign press had received too much other news from Hong Kong protesters and did not have time to explore other news that Hong Kong protesters did not tell them …

After that, Yau and Leung were reported to have difficulty in looking for a new job. Apparently, they both were not loved by Hong Kong employers.

* P.S. there have been multiple anti-government Hong Kong locals working as lawmakers in Hong Kong government, as long as they get sufficient votes from the public. One extreme example was Leung Kwok-hung (also called 'Long Hair'), who was jailed for anti-government actions before that. Another extreme example was Albert Ho Chun-yan, who was previously not granted travel documents to mainland China. There have been seats from pro-democratic individuals in the Hong Kong government. You really can't say Hong Kong have no democracy. At least, before 2019-20 protests …

3. Hong Kong locals who are against the protests

Within the Hong Kong community, it is publicly known that the protests were supported by about 50% of the community, and at the same time opposed by another 50% of the community. It was very different from Beijing students in 1989 who were supported by almost all Chinese citizens with only government leaders against them.

Refer to Supporting/References #1

Let us watch an interview with a 70-year-old woman, who was clearing bricks and barriers protesters had put on a busy road to paralyse traffic.
https://www.youtube.com/watch?v=TQcmnynfATE

In the interview, this retired woman expressed her anger about young protesters' throwing bricks, attacking police officers. She also complained that many press media in Hong Kong do not broadcast interviews against the protests.

Refer to Surprising Facts: 'Why are Hong Kong people angry about the Hong Kong government and/or China before 2019 protests' - Section 7 'Press media'

The protest received even less support from Hong Kong locals since they have gone violent, and the unrest persists infinitely even after the extradition bill which sparked the protests has already been withdrawn in Oct-19. In the beginning, protest activists accused police of disguising protesters to damage public facilities; but in later stages of the protests, it became undebatable that certain damages, if not all, were committed by protesters. Some of my pro-democratic Hong Kong ex-colleagues put on Facebook posts to condemn the violence of protesters.

Hong Kong locals who go against the protests do not necessarily hate democracy or love the Chinese government. They are against the protests because protesters use the fight for democracy as a justification to break the laws (eg. violence, injuring police officers and pro-government individuals, damaging public facilities and not paying train fares as a 'punishment' to pro-government public transport operators). Hong Kong locals are also unhappy about the financial, emotional and relationship damages the protests bring. Some are against the protests because this 'pro-democracy movement' itself is not democratic.

Source: Social media of Hong Kong locals, video interviews with Hong Kong locals in Cantonese news.

In social media, Hong Kong newspapers and the Internet, it is not difficult to find pro-government Hong Kong citizens (usually older generations) calling protest activists '廢青' (rubbish youngsters) and '黃屍' (yellow umbrella the corpses). Soon, protesters fight back and call pro-government Hong Kong citizens '廢老' (rubbish elderly).

Refer to Surprising facts: 'Why had older generations who oppose the protests rarely spoken out to foreign governments or the foreign press?'

Refer to Surprising facts: 'Why are protesters called '廢青' (rubbish youngsters) by mature Hong Kong locals?'

Those who oppose HK protests are predominantly the older generations who had witnessed the British colony Hong Kong and found there are pros and cons for both British and Chinese governments. Many are also unhappy that the unrest has been destroying business environments and stability of Hong Kong, as well as locals' personal safety and prosperities.

BBC news in traditional Chinese (Hong Kong language): '但香港社會也有人支持警察執法，對遊行中一些示威者的舉動表達不滿，擔憂香港穩定和繁榮 (But some of the Hong Kong community support the police to prosecute protesters. They are unhappy about the actions of protesters, worrying the protests would destroy the stability and prosperities of Hong Kong.) '

Source: https://www.bbc.com/zhongwen/trad/chinese-news-49110377

Let us watch Hong Kong crowds supporting Hong Kong police 撐警察 (to prosecute protesters for their illegal activities): https://www.youtube.com/watch?v=1ikOzSz9D5c

Description of the video '民間聲援警察集會 … 支持警方嚴正執法，並抗議近日有示威者衝擊警察的暴力行為。(Civilians supporting Hong Kong police and the prosecution of protesters. They also condemned protesters' violence and attacking police officers.) '

This campaign on 30-Jun-2019 was led by top pop-singers in the 1980s, Alan Tam and Kenny Bee. Tam and Bee had never been active in politics before this campaign. The crowd sang a song to encourage Hong Kong people to accept and support each other instead of attack each other violently.

In another video of the same campaign, 69-year-old Tam and few other Hong Kong celebrities said, 'We old people have witnessed the growth of Hong Kong. Without nomocracy, this city cannot possibly continue its success and prosperity.' 'Hong Kong police is amongst the most civilized and most protective to the people compared to other countries' 'Now the police are insulted and challenged (by protesters). (Protesters are) absolutely wrong!' 'We only want order and stability in society. That's it! But these few years (since the Umbrella Movement), our society has been gradually losing order and stability.'
https://www.youtube.com/watch?v=aumldELxdag

In later stages of the protests, as the Chinese government had not agreed to protesters' demands, protest leaders suggested the last hope of the protests was to seek support from Western countries such as the United States and the United Kingdom. Therefore, they pro-actively contacted the foreign press and foreign governments about their side of the story. In contrast, pro-government Hong Kong locals continue with their lives and expect the Chinese or Hong Kong government will do their job to combat the unrest anyway.

Quite a lot of Hong Kong locals do consider the protests as riots and wish the activists to be jailed.

Source: multiple Hong Kong discussion groups & social media

4. Hong Kong independence!!! Less than 20% of Hongkongers support it …

Before we start, you will ask, 'Crowds are crying 'Free Hong Kong', 'Liberate Hong Kong'. Why do you say only less than 20% of Hongkongers support Hong Kong independence?'

The primary slogan of the protests in traditional Chinese (Hong Kong language) is '光復香港'. Literately, '光' = 'shine, '復' = 'resurrect' or 'strong' or 'recover', '香港' = 'Hong Kong'.

So, slogan in Hong Kong language '光復香港' = 'Let Hong Kong shine and recover/strong again' has nothing to do to 'Free' or 'Liberate' in the English slogans.

Refer to Collins' dictionary. English translation of the vocabulary '光復' = 'recover', which has no implications of 'Free' nor 'Liberate': https://www.collinsdictionary.com/dictionary/chinese-english/%E5%85%89%E5%A4%8D

When the crowds join the protests, they see and support '光復香港 (Let Hong Kong shine and recover/strong again) '; but in English, protest leaders write it as 'Liberate Hong Kong' or 'Free Hong Kong', which has nothing to do to the traditional Chinese slogan, Hong Kong language. English-speaking countries are, therefore, under the impression that the crowds are protesting to 'Liberate Hong Kong' or 'Free Hong Kong', but traditional Chinese-reading Hongkongers believe they are supporting 'Let Hong Kong shine and recover/strong again'.

Protest leaders intentionally wrongly translate the slogans to mislead the foreign press and foreign governments to gain their supports.

It is not the only time protest leaders intentionally mislead the foreign press and foreign governments. **Joshua Wong and other protest leaders always speak to the foreign press and foreign governments as if they represent all Hong Kong people, while there are so many voices in Hong Kong against them. Protest leaders want to make foreign press and foreign governments believe Hong Kong people want independence. Then they would naturally become the new prime minister and new lawmakers of an independent Hong Kong.**

According to a survey conducted by The Chinese University of Hong Kong (CUHK) in July 2016, nearly 40% of Hongkongers aged 15 to 24 supported the territory becoming an independent country, whereas **17.4% of the overall respondents supported independence. 69.6% of respondents supported maintaining 'One Country, Two Systems'. Slightly over 13% of respondents supported direct governance by China.**

Source: Wiki. You can double-check the exact survey by The Chinese University of Hong Kong

What about the trend in 2019-20 in the time of Hong Kong protests? I interviewed more than 10 Hong Kong locals supporting the protests, all aged over 40. **NONE of the protesters I interviewed supported Hong Kong independence. They protest for one or some of the 5 key demands but DO NOT WANT HONG KONG TO GO INDEPENDENT.**

(I was unable to interview protesters aged under 40. Surely, according to TV news/videos, there are indeed a significant number of youngsters who want Hong Kong independence.)

Why do Hong Kong locals generally oppose independence? Let us analyse what will surely happen if Hong Kong goes independent:

- **Military**: Hong Kong does not have its own military. Hong Kong's military has been provided by the British when it was her colony and provided by China since 1997. Should Hong Kong become an independent country, it needs to have its own military.

  Look at a country of similar size, Singapore. All men in the country must join the army for at least 2 years. Every national day, Singapore shows off her fighter aircraft and tanks. Without a strong army, small countries with Hong Kong's size can easily be invaded by other powers.

  Military expenditure of an independent country is very expensive. Who is going to pay the bill? Taxpayers, of course. Going independent, Hong Kong would need to vastly increase taxes such as salary tax and impose GST as Singapore and other independent countries do. Hong Kong people are now unhappy with China mainly because they feel China is taking advantage of them economically and the Hong Kong government is wasting money on expensive contracts. Isn't it much worst to pay a large military bill instead???

  And do Hong Kong people want their men all compulsorily join the army for 2 years?

Refer to Surprising facts: 'Why are Hong Kong people angry about the Hong Kong government and/or China before 2019 protests?'

- **Tax rises**: As explained above.

- **Likely sanction by China:** Should Hong Kong go independent, it will surely offend China. Now China is economically strong and has many allies in the World. If China imposes sanctions to Hong Kong, Hong Kong will become another Cuba, which had been under sanctions by their strong neighbour, the United States.

- **Loss of businesses**: Some, but not all, foreigners invest in Hong Kong because of its ties with China. Losing the ties with China, Hong Kong definitely lose its advantages.

- **Terrible inflation**: Cheap vegetables, meats and other cheap goods sold in Hong Kong markets are from China. Without a business tie with China, Hong Kong can only get more expensive vegetables, meats and other food from other countries. Poorest people will suffer. Hong Kong people will also be unable to buy cheap products manufactured by China.

In conclusion, it is unrealistic for Hong Kong to seek independence. People must suffer much worse than today. Few people will surely be benefited from Hong Kong's independence – protest leaders, who will probably become the new prime minister and lawmakers of an independent Hong Kong.

5. Violent. Pride their fight for democracy, while murder the freedom of fellow Hong Kong citizens of different opinions

Let us watch a Hong Kong video: 市民憤怒了 市民：口講民主又唔見你問吓我 (Angry Hong Kong citizens said, '(Protesters) say democracy, but they did not consult me.') https://www.youtube.com/watch?v=MGtgLbUj9PQ

In the video (0:19), citizen Mr Chao said, 'Originally, I strongly supported this pro-democracy movement ... Not anymore, it is now damaging the livelihood of the people. It is definitely not what I would advocate.'

Video (0:34): the woman said, 'That terrible! I'm now furious! I have been stuck here for almost an hour!!!! (Do you agree on this movement or not?) No! Definitely not! Protesters need to give some time to let the government decide on the changes that they proposed. They can't expect everything to change instantly!!!! Protesters say democracy ... democracy. But have they even consulted me??? Why should I pay the price for something I do not need?'

(Please also note, the above video was posted in Jul-2019, far earlier than COVID19 outbreak in Dec-2019. Young people were wearing masks to hide their identities in the protests, but then they accuse police of disguising them to commit crimes. We will talk more about this later.)

I have interviewed a middle-aged Hong Kong citizen, she said the unrest has led to substantial pain to Hong Kong people, both mentally and financially. She said, 'It has been a painful year to both protesters and pro-government Hong Kong locals. Schools, personal lives and works are all badly impacted by the protests.'

According to her, many people do not support the protests, but protesters wanted more people to join their university strikes and work strikes. 'Protesters damages public transport, especially the busiest transportation hubs, to stop people from going to work. They want to force innocent people to join their strikes.'

She added, 'Schools and universities are badly affected too. Some university students want to attend lectures. But crazy protesters break into classrooms and scream for strikes, when lecturers are there, giving lectures. For high schools, those who want to continue their studies can only go to school to 'standby'. If a sufficient number of students attend school on a day, then lessons would go on; if not, everyone wastes their time for the day and go home.'

She said that many social gatherings need to be cancelled. 'The street is not safe. Those protesters are crazy. They throw bricks, bicycles and other things. The street is unsafe. Also, transports can be blocked anytime by the protesters. MTR stations are sometimes set on fire and closed. You can't tell whether a station is open or closed until you are there.'

Other Hong Kong locals said that taxi fares rise by 10 times after 10 pm as the road is unsafe and public transport is unavailable. 'If you are late, you would rather stay in a hotel than to go home,' another Hong Kong local said. If you know Hong Kong, normally, you should be able to go shopping at 11 pm as many shops in Mongkok and Causeway Bay are still open. Most restaurants close at 11 pm, but dessert restaurants are usually crowded at 12 am till 2 am.

The protests also bring financial damages to private companies. Many bankrupt. According to statistics, bankruptcy cases in Hong Kong rose by 19.86% per cent in October-December 2019 (4-6 months since the protests began), compared to the same period in 2018.

Source: https://www.oro.gov.hk/cgi-bin/oro/stat.cgi

While protesters say they fight for freedom, other Hong Kong locals who want to go on with their works, studies, businesses and social lives have unwillingly lost their freedom to live their normal lives.

Protesters feel that they are righteous and forces everyone in Hong Kong to follow them. Here are some examples of Hong Kong locals who oppose the protests, with usual responses from protesters:

- **Small shop owners in protest areas**: Rents in Hong Kong is the most expensive in the world (***Refer to Supporting/References #8***). With unrest continues, businesses are not only losing tourists but also losing local shoppers. But huge rents continue as rental contracts were signed. Busy shopping areas become war zones in the unrest. Shop owners hope the unrest to stop so that they do not need to go bankruptcy.
  Protesters respond that shop owners should stop being materialistic and should sacrifice their money, as protesters sacrifice their time and efforts. Protesters urge everyone in Hong Kong to sacrifice and support their actions because it is right and just to do so. I personally asked a few protesters how they felt about businesses getting bankrupt for their actions, they said I was devilish to ask this question.

- **Professionals**: professionals in financial services, logistics, trading, technology, professional services, etc... worry about losing jobs or salary reduction if the unrest continues. Foreign investors and China investors may **soon** avoid Hong Kong and invest in other countries instead.

Young, unworked protesters respond that if they do not protest, Hong Kong will **eventually** become a place with no democracy. Foreign investors and China investors will, therefore, **eventually** leave Hong Kong.

Source: conversations in Hong Kong discussion groups, traditional Chinese

Many have lost their freedom of speech too. If you can read traditional Chinese, you can see a lot of messages in Hong Kong discussion groups or social media of protesters verbally abusing pro-government Hong Kong people.

Let us watch a video (a man surrounded by gangsters and was set on fire for having different political views). **Warning: this video is highly offensive and was deleted by Youtube for multiple times, according to Youtube discussion** https://www.youtube.com/watch?v=24uhVYrE1ho&feature=yo utu.be&bpctr=1598244024

Video (2:32): the man said, '(You all speak as if) you all are not Chinese!'
A female voice replied, '(We are) Hong Kong people!!!!'
Then they set the man on fire.

(P.S. That man said Hong Kong people are Chinese because the vast majority of Hong Kong people are descendants of Chinese immigrants. Chinese immigrants moved to Hong Kong, Singapore and other Southeast Asian countries due to wars, civil wars, famine and cultural revolution from 1841 to 1980. Hong Kong's population increased from 7.45 thousand in the year 1841 when it became a British Colony to 6.4 million in 1996 when it returns to China, predominately due to the influx of Chinese immigrants.

However, after a few generations, some of today's Hong Kong youngsters deny they are Chinese – they forget their ancestors.)

Hong Kong protesters pride themselves for pursuing a precious value, democracy, and accuse those who do not support them as 'idiots', 'evil' or 'bribed'. You can frequently see these in Hong Kong discussion groups, unfortunately in traditional Chinese (Hong Kong language). Both pro-government Hongkongers and protesters are attacking each other, both verbally and physically. But from what I notice, protesters are relatively ruder and more emotional in verbal assaults.

In the protests, there are complaints on physical assaults by triads, police and protesters. It is not surprising triads and police would physically attack (I don't mean they are right), but it is worrying that civilian protesters are physical attacking police and other civilians (pro-government Hong Kong locals). In the beginning, protesters declared that the violence was committed by policemen disguising protesters. However, in later stages, evidence on violence committed by protesters was solid.

21-Jun-2019 marked the date when the peaceful protests turned into violent unrest. Let us watch how it happened: https://m.youtube.com/watch?v=KSkZ3yEFQsw

Video (0:00): Protesters throw umbrellas, bricks, metals towards police. Police protected themselves with their shields.
Video (0:50): Police could not stand the attack. They moved backward.
Video (2:30): A native English speaker on the scene tells what he saw in the building. Video (3:55) A legislator accused the police of entering the governmental building without proper permission. He said their injury was a ridiculous excuse for entering the governmental building.
Video (4:26): The police fought back.
Video (4:53): An old Hong Kong local man (a government officer) tells what he witnessed on that day. 'Before around 2:50 pm, it has been a peaceful demonstration. Protesters were singing, crying slogans and listening to government officials who supported the protests. Police and protesters did not have many interactions – I was glad they were peaceful, as I have been worrying about any clashes. Unfortunately, at around 2:50 pm, things changed dramatically. (Video 5:35): A group of masked men with helmet dragged up hundreds of bricks and transported constructional metal

sticks to the scene. At around 3:00 pm, these men started to attack (the police). Bricks, metal sticks and other trashes were throwing towards the police troop. I was up in the building and was terrified – at that time, the police only had shields and short police sticks. They could not possibly stand the attack! Soon, the police were defeated! After that, they came in and upgraded their equipment. The Special Tactical Squad also came to help.' 'To be honest, the majority of the protesters in the scene were peaceful. Only a small portion were rioters.'

Let us watch another video on the damages by rioters:
(The provider of this video intended to reveal the stupidity of protesters; but the focus of this quote is about the crimes they committed.)
https://www.youtube.com/watch?v=z0KXysIZFVE

Please note, the above video was posted in Oct-2019, far earlier than COVID19 outbreak in Dec-2019. Protesters were wearing masks to hide their identities, but then they accuse police of disguising them to commit crimes.

Regarding protesters' accusation that police officers disguising them to commit crimes, let us watch this video:
https://www.youtube.com/watch?v=iLu2lRGLHgc

Aren't these rioters too young to be policemen? Also, policemen must look at least slightly muscular because they are physically trained. What do you say?

There are not many reports on pro-government civilians physically attacking protesters.

You may ask, with such level of violence, why are so many Hong Kong locals still supporting the protests? First, some pro-protest civilians do not believe these videos. They feel that these videos are either acted by paid actors or by policemen disguising violent protesters.

Pro-protest civilians do not trust China. Since the 1989 Tiananmen incident, some just do not trust the Chinese government. Also, being educated about the beauty of democratic countries, pro-protest civilians do not trust governments of other forms.

In contrast, pro-government civilians do not believe the Chinese government or the Hong Kong government would harm Hong Kong people because Hongkongers and Chinese are the same race. Also, Hong Kong has been returned to China permanently, not temporarily. What are the benefits for China to harm a part of itself?

Second, press media play an important role in the Hong Kong protests. There are more than 30 newspapers, few radio stations and few television broadcasting companies in Hong Kong. Some are considered to be anti-government, also called '黃媒 (yellow umbrella press media)'. Example of 'yellow umbrella press media' includes Apple Daily, Stand News and Passion Times. Some other press media are considered to be pro-government. The rest are supposed to be neutral or unknown.

Anti-government press, pro-government press and neutral press report news very differently. There have been allegations that 'yellow umbrella press media' chop away how rioters start the attacks against the police and civilians. They only report latter part of the stories when the police attack back and violently arrest rioters. Examples are the above 21-Jun-2019 attack, the Prince Edward station attack and Yuen Long attack.

Some civilians only trust anti-government press media, because they feel that their news reporting against the government means they are fearless and therefore are most loyal to the people. The root cause is, again, the trust issue between the people and the government.

Watch this video about biased news reporting from either side: press:
https://m.facebook.com/story.php?story_fbid=2985998508084115&id=204990132851647

Talking about censorship, one may think of China or other conservative countries. However, in reality, not only governments can conduct censorship. Any news organizations, such as anti-government press media, can also conduct censorship.

Anti-government groups are especially pro-active in contacting foreign press and foreign governments as they want to gain support. It is why foreign countries are more likely to receive biased videos from anti-government press media. Look at the Amazon catalogue, almost all books about Hong Kong protests are against Hong Kong/Chinese governments. This book may be the only exception.

Third, most horrifyingly, some pro-protest civilians feel it is justified to violently attack the police and other civilians if the government is not as righteous as they wish. Since 2014 Umbrella movement, Joshua Wong and other Hong Kong protest leaders have been advocating that it is correct for civilians to engage in illegal activities if the government do not listen to the people.

In 2019, I had talked to a young ex-colleague in Hong Kong. She said, 'The government does not listen to the people when they are peaceful! How can we possibly make the government listen to us without violence?????'

Some Hong Kong locals have condemned protest leaders' ruining people's mind for justifying illegal activities when the government is not as righteous as they desire.

In fact, some pro-government civilians do not agree Hong Kong has no democracy. At least, before the 2019-20 protests. (Source: interviews with Hong Kong celebrities and Hong Kong civilians on the Internet) Everyone used to be able to tell their own views about the government or about anything. But since 2019 protests, speaking against either side can lead to attack by people with different opinions.

Each democratic country has a different type of democracy. The election system of Australia is different from that of the United States or Canada. The United Kingdom is a democratic country, but it has a queen. Each country has a different political system. Hong Kong does not need to copy from another country in order to be democratic. And which country has the best democratic system for Hong Kong to copy from? Canada? The United States? The United Kingdom? Australia? Singapore? Taiwan? At least, some Hong Kong locals do feel Hong Kong has a certain degree of democracy.

It would be best if Hong Kong enhances to have 'One man, one vote' for the Chief Executive, but it is not the sole indicator of democracy. Everyone in Hong Kong has a vote on who can get a seat in the legislative council to speak for them. Anti-government activists have been getting seats in the legislative council ... at least before 2019-20 protests. And Hong Kong people have the right to protest and speak in front of foreign press ... at least before 2019-20 protests. It is good to fight for more democracy, but do we need to violently attack each other for this purpose?

In Hong Kong/Chinese language, democracy = 民主, 民 = civilian, 主 = God/the lord/the decision-maker. In Hong Kong, pro-democracy activists interpret 'democracy' as 'civilians are the lords/decision-makers'. They feel, 'I am a civilian. Therefore, I am the lord/decision-maker and the government must listen to me. I should be the decision-maker on who governs us and what are the best government policies.' But they forget the fact that everyone in society is a civilian and everyone's opinions need to be considered.

Democracy means civilians **connectively** make decisions on what are the best to their society, not each civilian **individually** makes decisions on what himself/herself considers to be the best to the society and expect the government and everyone else in the community to follow him/her. The 'democracy' that Hong Kong protest activists are advocating does not have much difference from 'individualism'.

According to 'A Theory of Human Motivation' by Abraham Maslow, physiological needs, safety needs and love and belonging have to be satisfied before the pursue of self-actualization such as democracy. If a city like Hong Kong needs to sacrifice laws and orders, stability and prosperities for a pursue of democracy, then not many sensible people would choose democracy.

Now about 50% of Hong Kong locals are against the Hong Kong unrest, but the so-called 'pro-democracy activists' insist on their actions because they feel they are more righteous than the others. This alone makes this unrest not qualified as democratic movements.

There are different types of democracy, such as majoritarian democracy, consensus democracy and constitutional democracy. In layman term (and as I can understand as a layman), no matter which type of democracy one would prefer, democracy is to ensure everyone's voices are considered and agreements to be reached based on majority, consensus or law. Hong Kong pro-democracy activists feel that everyone should obey them because they are more righteous than the government and other members of society. It is just another form of **dictatorship**.

If Western countries accept these Hong Kong protest activists as asylum seekers, it would encourage violence and illegal activities in Hong Kong with no penalty. Any rioters in Hong Kong would believe it is justified for them to commit violent crimes as they will be protected by Western countries as long as they say they are fighting for democracy. Western countries would not only waste precious resources to support and award these young Hong Kong dictators by granting them permanent residency. They would also absorb bad members who would probably justify violence and radicalism again and destroy their new countries.

Should the pursuit of democracy be considered more important than laws and order, prosperities and the welfare and human rights of other members of a community? It is not the value that we should educate our younger generations.

6. Destructive, anti-social behaviour

2019 Hong Kong movement frontline activist, **Denise Ho Wan-see**, posted in her Facebook, '香港政府最緊張係經濟，大家應該要集中火力，從癱瘓銀行、大型機構、機場、交通工具、之類入手。同埋唔好等星期三先做，聽日就要開始。'
('Hong Kong government is most concerned about Hong Kong economy. We must focus on paralysing banks, enterprises, airports, public transports, etc… Don't only go on strike for 1 day on Wednesday. Let's start the strike from tomorrow. ')

Source: Denise's Facebook post on 10-Jun-2019:
https://www.facebook.com/HOCCHOCC/posts/101619854813
05230/

P.S., Denise holds Canadian Citizenship, though she was born in Hong Kong in 1977. She has been an activist in both 2014 Hong Kong Umbrella Movement and 2019 Hong Kong protests.

Now you understand why many Hong Kong locals hate this 'democratic movement'. It also explains why the Chinese government warns against foreign interference in Hong Kong in the protests.

After the introduction of the new national security law, Denise is still living in Hong Kong without being jailed or the need to flee to Canada, at least as of the time of writing. You really cannot say Hong Kong has no freedom of speech.

Another anti-social behaviour in the Hong Kong 2019-20 protests, some protesters advocate '攬炒' (Let us die/lose together).

The idea of '攬炒' is that some Hong Kong protesters feel that important values or lifestyles in Hong Kong have been destroyed. They feel that the government is not going to agree on their demands, so they are losers anyway. They would rather everyone in Hong Kong loses than only themselves lose. They implement '攬炒' by destroying the city and the people.

Other protesters advocated '攬炒' because they feel that they get nothing when Hong Kong is wealthy and stable. They would rather all 'die/lose together' to restart the city, see they may perhaps get something.

Source: Hong Kong netizens in discussion groups, in traditional Chinese.

Refer to Surprising facts: ' 攬炒' (Let's die/lose together) – a hot topic in Hong Kong since 2019 protests'

While '攬炒' is believed to be advocated by only some of Hong Kong protesters, 'leaders' in Hong Kong protests have failed to lead protesters to correct directions and stop destructive derivations from the movement.

And are these related to 'democracy' or 'human rights' at all?

7. Hong Kong protest student leaders are NOT top students, not even close

Copying from the 1989 Beijing protest, Hong Kong student leaders prided themselves as university graduates, more educated than the older generations.

In fact, however, Hong Kong's situation is very different from Beijing in 1989. In 1989, only very few small portions of people in China could go to University. In 1989, many people in China were illiterate. Also, Tsinghua University and Beijing University that protesting student leaders were studying were the top 2 universities in China.

In contrast, the student 'leader' in Hong Kong protests, **Joshua Wong**, was graduated from The Open University of Hong Kong (ranks #8 out of 8 in Hong Kong, the worst university). Other key activists, **Nathan Law** and **Yau Wai-ching,** were graduated from Lingnan University (ranks #7 out of 8 in Hong Kong, the 2nd worst). **Agnes Chow** was the best academically amongst Hong Kong protest leaders, graduated from Baptist University of Hong Kong (ranks #6 out of 8 in Hong Kong, the 3rd worst).

Many Hong Kong people have master's degrees. From my personal experience, around 1 out of 15 people middle-aged people I encountered in Hong Kong has master's degrees.

Considering around one in two young people in Hong Kong go to universities, with a high number of master's degree holders, getting bachelor's degrees in the worst 2 or 3 universities are really mediocre.

So why did Joshua name his ex-political group 'Scholarism'? Perhaps he wished to appear as a scholar?

Even Hong Kong's oldest generation is educated. Zero per cent of Hongkongers are illiterate.
Source: https://www.macrotrends.net/countries/HKG/hong-kong/literacy-rate

9 years' compulsory education has been in effect for more than 40 years. All Hong Kong locals at or under 40 years' old must have at least junior high school level. To my experience, elderlies at the age of 60-70 years' old typically have at least primary school levels. Almost all, if not all, of Hong Kong people born locally can understand at least basic English.

Refer to Supporting/References #2, #3

In other words, Beijing protesters in 1989 were best of the best academically in China's a billion population; while Hong Kong protest leaders are medium academically in the much smaller Hong Kong's 7 million population.

In 1989, top students in a billion' population gave up their beautiful future, sacrifice themselves for the benefits of all people in China; As for 2019-20 Hong Kong protests, students who marginally got their spots at the worst universities in Hong Kong see no future for themselves. They encourage unrest, allow violence, damage public facilities and private companies, destroy the stability of their community, hoping to build a new government and probably they can become prime ministers or senators. If the movement fails, they will be qualified to become asylum seekers in foreign countries, much easier than getting skill migration visas considering their terrible academic achievements. Appearing as leaders of Hong Kong, they will be loved by foreign employers and get good jobs. Good ideas for them!

Take Nathan Law as an example, he was admitted to Yale University for post-graduate studies in 2019 despite he was graduated from the 2nd worst university in Hong Kong. Thanks to his 'outstanding' performances in the 2014 Umbrella Movement and other 'contributions' to Hong Kong. Sadly, foreigners did not know 50% of Hong Kong locals hate his ruining their community. Yale University did believe Nathan was a super-leader or hero ... Sounds rewarding!

Nathan started his study at Yale University in Aug-2019 when he and his teams were asking Hong Kong students to go on university strikes for the 2019-20 protests.

8. Protest activists had never experienced Hong Kong as a British colony

If you watch TV news on Hong Kong protests, you will notice the majority of protesters are around 20 years old or even younger. Ex-British colony Hong Kong became a part of China 23 years ago (on 01-Jul-1997). Most of these protesters were not even born.

Looking at the most famous Hong Kong protest activists, Joshua Wong was less than 1 year old when the ex-British Colony became a part of China. Another activist, Nathan Law, was born in China and only moved to Hong Kong 2 years after Hong Kong became a part of China.

Source: According to Wiki, Joshua Wong was born on 13-October-1996, and Nathan Law was born on 13-July-1993 in Shenzhen, China. Nathan has a Hong Kong father and a Mainland Chinese mother. He moved to Hong Kong with his mother for a family reunion when he was around six.

Older generations, who had witnessed both Hong Kong as a British colony and Hong Kong as Special Administrative Region (HKSAR) of China, are relatively less supportive of the protests. In contrast, young protest leaders and young protesters believe Hong Kong would have been better if it is still a British colony (or as democratic), but themselves have not actually experienced it.

9. Facing financial bankruptcy

As mentioned earlier, Hong Kong protest activists Yau Wai-ching and Baggio Leung were disqualified for unwillingness to speak the oath as lawmakers in 2016. They were unhappy about being disqualified for this reason and appealed twice to the highest court. They lost the lawsuits and needed to repay the legal fees, salaries and allowances on unworked days to Hong Kong Legislative Council.

Newspaper dated 11-May-2018:
https://www.scmp.com/news/hong-kong/hong-kong-law-and-crime/article/2145676/under-threat-jail-and-bankruptcy-baggio-leung

Facing bankruptcy, Yau responded: '自己本身不是有錢人', '破產咪破產囉無所謂'. ('Go bankrupt then. Not a problem.' 'Afterall, I have never been rich.')

Source:
https://news.modia.com.hk/2017/08/24/35219/%E6%B8%B8%E8%95%99%E7%A6%8E%EF%BC%9A%E9%9D%A2%E8%87%A8%E7%A0%B4%E7%94%A2%E9%9D%9E%E5%9B%B0%E5%A2%83-%E5%95%8F%E5%AE%B6%E4%BA%BA%E6%94%9E%E9%8C%A2%E6%84%9F%E6%84%A7%E7%96%9A/

Perhaps Yau was right. If she and Leung go bankrupt, it won't be a problem for her. The bill will be covered by the creditor, Hong Kong government - taxpayers' money!

And have they ever considered their chances to win the lawsuits and possible consequences before their actions???? Isn't it common sense that important positions with a requirement to speak the oath will make them disqualified if they are unwilling to do so? Not many pitied them for losing such lawsuits and losing their positions.

Under regulations in many developed countries, bankrupt individuals are not allowed to take important positions such as company director. However, Yau and Leung had been activists in 2019-20 protests.

According to the latest news just a few days before this book was published, Hong Kong Legislative Council will ask the courts to declare Leung bankrupt. The Council has not made Yau bankrupt as she had made recommendations on how she hoped to repay the amount.
https://www.msn.com/en-sg/news/world/bankruptcy-ruling-sought-as-disqualified-hong-kong-lawmaker-baggio-leung-fails-to-repay-hkdollar930000-owed-to-legislature/ar-BB16r53e?li=AAavKXU

10. 47-66% of Hong Kong locals opposed the extradition bill which sparked the violent protests

The below surveys were conducted before the 2019 Hong Kong protests.

According to the survey by The Chinese University of Hong Kong, 47% Hong Kong locals opposed to the extradition bill. The survey was 'Do you agree or disagree with the extradition bill now proposed by the (Hong Kong) government?' 「支持定反對政府現時提出的《逃犯條例》修訂草案」

According to another survey by the University of Hong Kong, 66% of Hong Kong locals opposed to the extradition bill. This survey was 'Do you agree Hong Kong citizens be extradited for a hearing in China? 「把香港人引渡去內地受審」

Please note: the two surveys gave different outcomes as the questions were different.

Source:
https://theinitium.com/article/20190613-opinion-francislee-fugitive-offenders-ordinance/

https://www.hkcnews.com/article/21065/%E9%80%83%E7%8A%AF%E6%A2%9D%E4%BE%8B-%E6%B8%AF%E5%A4%A7%E6%B0%91%E8%AA%BF-%E7%A7%BB%E6%B0%91-21065/%E6%B8%AF%E5%A4%A7%E6%B0%91%E8%AA%BF%EF%BC%9A%E9%80%BE%E5%9B%9B%E6%88%90%E4%BA%BA%E6%8C%87%E8%8B%A5%E5%BC%95%E6%B8%A1%E4%BF%AE%E4%BE%8B%E9%80%9A%E9%81%8E-

%E8%80%83%E6%85%AE%E7%A7%BB%E6%B0%91%E6%
88%96%E8%BD%89%E7%A7%BB%E8%B3%87%E7%94%A2

I don't mean 47-66% is low, but with such large-scale and violent unrest, probably it is lower than how foreigners may think?

According to another Hong Kong newspaper, 700 thousands of Hong Kong citizens had joined a poll on the Internet to support the extradition bill. To ensure credibility, another 130 thousands unnamed signature supporting the bill had been excluded from the poll, the report said. In this report, two solicitors (one is a basic law committee member) had also explained why they supported the bill. 20 fisherman boats also protested to support the bill:

https://topick.hket.com/article/2372246/%E3%80%90%E9%80
%83%E7%8A%AF%E6%A2%9D%E4%BE%8B%E3%80%91
%E4%BF%9D%E5%85%AC%E7%BE%A9%E6%92%90%E4
%BF%AE%E4%BE%8B%E5%A4%A7%E8%81%AF%E7%9B
%9F%E3%80%80%E6%94%B6%E9%9B%8670%E8%90%AC
%E7%B0%BD%E5%90%8D%E6%94%AF%E6%8C%81%E4
%BF%AE%E4%BE%8B

There have been no similar reports by the foreign press found on the Internet. Foreign news generally reported as if all Hong Kong locals were against the bill.

Within the Hong Kong community, it had been widely agreed that some Hong Kong locals did support the extradition bill, some very well-educated.

I had interviewed a few Hong Kong locals. My ex-senior manager in an International bank currently in Hong Kong supported the bill. He was graduated from a top university in the United Kingdom. Another lady in dental services also supported the bill. It was not because they love the contents of the bill, but they feel that the world is ever-changing and sometimes it is necessary to introduce new laws as a civilised society. As they do not believe the bill has a real problem and can see why the bill is reasonable, they would like to support their government.

11. Protesters: True violation of Sino-British Joint Declaration: 'One country, two systems'

One of the major justifications by the protesters was that they feel China has violated the 'Sino-British Joint Declaration' signed between the United Kingdom and China on the transfer of sovereignty of Hong Kong to China.

In the agreement, 'One country, two systems' enables Hong Kong to keep its capitalist system for 50 years, from 1997 to 2047. They call it 五十年不變 (no change for 50 years). Hong Kong SAR of China would not practise the socialist system in mainland China for 50 years, from 1997 to 2047.

In TV news, you can frequently see Hong Kong protester raising the slogan of 'Hong Kong independence' or 'Free Hong Kong'. These demands are clear violations of the Sino-British Joint Declaration. Hong Kong protesters have been focusing to defend 'two systems' in the Sino-British Joint Declaration, but often forget 'one country' in the same agreement.

Refer to: Surprising facts: 'Sino-British Joint Declaration/ Hong Kong Basic Law'

Also refer to: Surprising facts: 'False hopes of the protests: Only 50 years unchanged'

12. Protesters joining the democratic movement for anger over China

The primary slogan of the protest is '光復香港' ('Let Hong Kong shine and recover/strong again').

I have read Facebook posts from pro-protest friends in Hong Kong and essays by pro-protest groups in 2019-2020. When protesters try to persuade other Hong Kong locals to join the protests, their arguments are almost always about the soaring housing prices in Hong Kong, lives in Hong Kong becoming difficult, uneducated Chinese immigrants to Hong Kong taking up social welfare, the influx of Chinese tourists leading to inflation and over-crowding, government spending too much money on over-priced infrastructures, wasting taxpayers' money. One example is the expensive Hong Kong-Zhuhai-Macao Bridge, which many Hong Kong people feel that the construction costs Hong Kong taxpayers too much but mainly benefit China (Zhuhai and Macao).

Refer to Surprising facts: 'Problems in Hong Kong society before 2019 protests'

Refer to Surprising facts: 'Why are Hong Kong people angry about the Hong Kong government and/or China before 2019 protests?'

Many protesters are protesting because they are unhappy with policies and how the government spend taxpayers' money. They may not be wrong ... but, is it really a democratic movement?

13. Hong Kong government had tolerated the violent protests and instability of Hong Kong for 8 months before imposing the new national security law

2019 Hong Kong protests were initiated by the extradition bill in Jun-19. The government agreed to withdraw the bill in Oct-19, yet protests (and violence) continued as protesters raised few additional big demands since the protest began.

Some of the 5 key demands of the protesters are indeed vast and difficult to implement. Some of them impose high risks to the sovereignty of China over Hong Kong, which may eventually lead to the collapse of 'One country, two systems'. Also, bear in mind, the protesters supported by 50% of their community are, at the same time, opposed by another 50% of the community. Even in democratic countries, parliaments cannot pass a referendum if 50% for and 50% against.

Protesters say, 五大訴求, 缺一不可 (Five demands, no one less). The 5 demands are:

I) Full withdrawal of the extradition bill

Outcome: Hong Kong government had agreed to this demand in Oct-19.

II) A commission of inquiry into alleged police brutality

Analysis: Before looking into the matter, let us revisit why protesters were arrested:
https://www.youtube.com/watch?v=iLu2lRGLHgc

Also, critics say that this demand can be very hard to implement. Unlike George Floyd's case which has only 1 victim and few policemen around, there had been so many unrests.
You may choose to form a different opinion on this.

In recent Hong Kong protests from 2014, there has been plenty of accusation of arbitrary detention or unnecessary violence by Hong Kong police in pro-democracy protests. Before that, the Hong Kong police had been having very good reputations. So, the idea of the accusation is that all the 29,000 Hong Kong policemen/policewomen suddenly turn evil because of the protests … Protesters seem to feel that policemen/policewomen have political interests to protect the government from going more democratic …

Assuming arbitrary detention does occur in the protests, somehow it never happens to protest leaders. Look at Joshua Wong, Nathan Law, Agnes Chow, Jimmy Lai and Denise Ho – somehow they could not be arbitrarily arrested without the introduction of the new national security law.

On the other hand, it appears that Joshua Wong has been having a credibility problem even before 2019 protests which started in July:

https://www.scmp.com/news/hong-kong/law-and-crime/article/2183681/hong-kong-activist-joshua-wong-made-claims-he-had-squat

III) Retracting the classification of protesters as 'rioters'

Analysis: Many other Hong Kong locals also call those protesters 'rioters'.

Let us watch Hong Kong crowds shouting at protesters, calling them 暴徒(rioters):
https://www.youtube.com/watch?v=E0i0aFPISD4

Background of this video: protesters were blocking train doors, stopping trains from moving and paralysing the entire train track. They wanted to force innocent people to join their strike. Angry Hong Kong locals call them rioters. Many Hong Kong locals also call protesters 甲由(cockroaches) because they are in black, damaging enterprises, public facilities, harming innocent people and sneaking around everywhere.

According to the Cambridge dictionary, 'rioter' is defined as one of a group of people who meet in a public place and behave in a noisy, violent and uncontrolled way, often as a protest.

In other words, if Hong Kong/Chinese governments do not use a different definition of 'rioters' from Cambridge dictionary or similar, then this demand is considered unsatisfied and the unrest will continue under protesters' 'Five demands, no one less' declaration …

IV) Amnesty for arrested protesters

Analysis: This is an unconditional demand. Even for protesters who attack the police (or other human beings) or destroy public or private facilities are requested to be amnestied in this demand.

It may protest human rights of protesters; but what about human rights of those people who had been attacked?

And should this demand be satisfied, is Hong Kong still a place with nomocracy?

V) Dual universal suffrage, meaning for both the Legislative Council and the Chief Executive

Explanation: Currently, the Chief Executive (equivalent to a prime minister or a governor) is elected by a 1200-member committee. These 1200 people are elected by Hong Kong people. In other words, currently, only those people who are elected by the people has the power to elect the Chief Executive of Hong Kong. Furthermore, it has been believed that some of these 1200 people may be controlled by the Chinese government.

Now, this demand is to fight for 'one man, one vote' in the election for the Chief Executive.

Previously, Hong Kong people had been under the belief that 'one man, one vote' for the Chief Executive would be implemented in 2008. However, the government later clarified that it had never been agreed in Sino-British Joint Declaration nor Hong Kong Basic Law. This claim seemed to be valid according to those documents.

Refer to Surprising Facts: 'Election of Chief Executive of Hong Kong – Controversies and Glory'

It is worth to mention that Hong Kong citizens had never got 'one man, one vote' to the governor even in the time as a British colony.

Protesters declared that the protests would continue if the government does not agree on ALL of the above 5 big and difficult demands. Same as the attitude toward the protests, many pro-government Hong Kong locals feel that some of the 5 big demands are unrealistic or unreasonable.

With unrest continued for another 8 months and Hong Kong government cannot agree to all 5 big demands, China eventually imposed the new security law to Hong Kong. While it is true that the new security Law reduces freedom of speech, but the question is: can the unrest possibly end without the new security law? There are, indeed, about 50% of the Hong Kong community have been against the protests and eager to get their lives back to normal.

14. Discrimination against Hong Kong immigrants to other countries

Protest activists pride themselves of 'willing to sacrifice everything for Hong Kong', 'ready to be punished for the protest' and 'truly love Hong Kong'. There had been occasional criticism from protesters, accusing Hong Kong immigrants to other countries as 'not truly loving Hong Kong' and 'consuming Hong Kong resources and leave'.

Source: Hong Kong discussion groups, social media, in traditional Chinese

But now, protest activists change and want to flee Hong Kong. They changed from 'ready to bear the consequences' to 'I don't want to be jailed', as they now say in foreign TV news interviews. They now seek to become immigrants to other countries as asylum seekers, while themselves and their followers had been laughing at Hong Kong immigrants to other countries just a few months ago.

According to TV news in Australia, more than 60 Hong Kong protest activists are believed to be in overseas' countries, seeking asylum, since the proposal of the new security law.

In a TV interview by SBS news, Australia, a Hong Kong protest leader is currently in Australia, seeking asylum. 'Australia is a country with democracy,' he smiled, 'I'd love to stay here!' leaving behind the mess to his supporters and damages to the whole Hong Kong community. Now all Hong Kong locals are paying the price of losing a certain level of freedom, financial damages, business losses and social instability, while protest leaders are now happily fleeing to your country.

In the same TV news interview, an analyst said that this Hong Kong protest leader is likely to be granted a permanent residency in Australia, given he has different political views from his own government and he may be jailed if he returns to Hong Kong. (But how did he get to a flight in Hong Kong airport without being jailed in the first place???) The analysis did not consider how much violence and damages he had bought to his community, despite opposition from other Hong Kong locals.

Perhaps violence, paralysing banks, enterprises, airports and public transports, killing others' businesses and damaging their community is a pathway to migrate to Australia, the United States, Canada and the United Kingdom? Sounds better than skilled migration and partner visas!

· **This book is about Hong Kong protest activists (asylum seekers), which is a different topic from whether safe haven should be given to the innocent Hong Kong general public.**

· **This book has not looked into all accusations against Hong Kong protest leaders. For example, there were accusations about their funding and alleged financial corruption.**

Surprising facts related to Hong Kong protests that you may or may not know

'攬炒' (Let's die/lose together) – a hot topic in Hong Kong since 2019 protests

Hong Kong pop jargon, '攬炒' had been used since 2019 protests began. See below essay dated 1-Sep-2019 which discuss the topic of '攬炒':

https://www.thestandnews.com/politics/%E6%89%80%E8%AC%82-%E6%94%AC%E7%82%92/

* Please note that the above is a pro-protests website

On 03-Dec-2019, username '我要攬炒' (I want to die/lose together) put a post in LIHKG discussion group (lihkg.com). Since then, '攬炒' has become a hot topic in Hong Kong, probably because many Hong Kong locals did agree the unrest would lead to '攬炒' (die/lose together) of Hong Kong.

Hong Kong top-tycoon, Li Ka-shing, publish on the front page of newspapers on 19-Aug-2019 against violence: '最好的因可成最壞的果' ('the best of intentions can lead to the worst outcome'). From there, you can see Hong Kong citizens had already foreseen the unrest would end tragically.

He added, 'Love freedom, Love tolerance, Love nomocracy… Love Hong Kong, Love China, Love yourself… from an ordinary Hong Kong Citizen, Li'

Chinese full version:

https://news.mingpao.com/ins/%E6%B8%AF%E8%81%9E/art
icle/20190816/s00001/1565915200271/%E3%80%90%E9%80%
83%E7%8A%AF%E6%A2%9D%E4%BE%8B%E3%80%91%E
6%9D%8E%E5%98%89%E8%AA%A0%E9%A6%96%E7%99
%BC%E8%81%B2-
%E6%9C%80%E5%A5%BD%E7%9A%84%E5%9B%A0%E5
%8F%AF%E6%88%90%E6%9C%80%E5%A3%9E%E7%9A%
84%E6%9E%9C

English version:

https://www.forbes.com/sites/daviddawkins/2019/08/16/hong-
kongs-richest-man-appeals-to-anti-government-protestors--stop-
the-violence/#239ad8575730

(About Li Ka-shing: Li was born in 1928 and has been a retiree since 10-May-2018. He had been the top tycoon in Hong Kong and Asia for years and had never been active in politics. He started working since he was 12 years' old. Later, he borrowed money from relatives to establish his own factory, and soon his business was very successful. He turned from a little nothing to become a top tycoon. He had been a role model to many in the 1980s and 1990s.)

The new national security law in Hong Kong was proposed by China on 22-May-2020. The above '攬炒' speeches were dated 01-Sep-2019 and Li's declaration was released in Aug-2019, far earlier than new national security law was suggested.

With the announcement of the New national security law, many Hong Kong locals say to the young protesters, '攬炒成功' (Now we successfully all die/lose together as you wished!!!)

Why are protesters called '廢青' (rubbish youngsters) by mature Hong Kong locals?

The word '廢青' became a pop jargon in Hong Kong since 2014 Umbrella Movement. For example, when Joshua Wong was found to have secretly taken syrup in his hunger strike, many Hong Kong netizens called him '廢青'. Since then, the word '廢青' is frequently seen in Hong Kong's local newspapers, discussion groups and social media. It is a Hong Kong pop Jargon, not generally used in mainland China.

In the past 30 years, Hong Kong has been well-developed and wealthy. It has been very prevalent for families to hire domestic helpers from the Philippines, Indonesia or Thailand. Youngsters grew up in the hand of domestic helpers in the past 20 years, with their parents both worked full time and had little time to look after them.

When these children grew up, they had long been criticized to have little ability to take care of themselves as they just needed to say a word to make domestic helpers do everything for them. For example, there had been reports that children aged 8 years' old did not know how to shower themselves. Other reports stated that some children aged 10 years' old did not know how to tie their shoes …

Being too wealthy, and because hard-working parents spoiled them much when those parents only had little time with them, these children grew up in an environment that expensive, luxury items came easily.

Now, these children become young adults. They suddenly realise it is not as easy to get the expensive luxury items they had always had. These require their hard work. What has changed? Why has life become so difficult? Instead of improving their work skills and working hard as their parents did, youngsters feel that the difficult environment can be due to the fact that Hong Kong is now governed by communist China instead of the democratic British.

Older generations of Hong Kong feel that these young adults do not do their own jobs to work hard or find business opportunities to thrive in the ever-changing world. Some also blame the youngers for their failure to judge what is right and what is wrong, such as putting all the blames to the government for their own failure in their job seeking or gaining good salaries. Young, unworked protesters feel heroic to fight for precious values, democracy, and blame the older generations for being materialistic and not dare to confront the 'evil communist'.

Please note, the word '廢青' is only used to refer to young protesters in Hong Kong protests, including Umbrella Movement (2014) and Hong Kong unrest (2019-20). '廢青' is not normally used to refer to a general youngster in Hong Kong.

Why had older generations who oppose the protests rarely spoken out to foreign governments or the foreign press?

Hong Kong older generations who oppose the protests are less likely to speak out to foreign countries. Here are the reasons:

1) **Language barriers.**

   Native English-speaking teachers are only introduced into Hong Kong schools in recent 30 years or so. Older Hong Kong locals' English was taught by local Hong Kong teachers, who have a strong accent. Spoken English by older Hong Kong locals cannot always be understood by native English speakers. Some older Hong Kong locals do not dare to speak in English when native speakers cannot usually understand them.

   All Hong Kong people born locally can understand at least basic written English.

2) **They are not protesting on the street, and therefore unlikely to be caught by foreign journalists for interviews**

   In the unrest, streets can become war-zones at any time. Pro-government locals normally avoid the streets which are likely to have protests and therefore are not caught by the foreign press for interviews.

3) **No need to speak out**

   They believe the government will do the work to combat the protest anyway. They don't even think it is necessary to speak out.

4) Too dangerous to speak out

Not only speaking against the Chinese government is dangerous, speaking against the protests can be equally dangerous when many have gone violent. I originally planned to go to Hong Kong for personal reasons in late 2019, but my relatives and friends in Hong Kong told me not to go, for fear I would be heavily injured if I say something against the protests in the public.

5) Many did speak out

Some older Hong Kong locals did make public declaration to urge the youngsters to stop the unrests. Famous people include actor Jackie Chan, actress Kathy Chow Hoi-Mei and retiree top-tycoon Li Ka-shing, amongst the others.
https://www.cnbc.com/2019/08/16/hong-kong-protests-tycoon-li-ka-shing-urges-love-not-violence.html

https://www.forbes.com/sites/daviddawkins/2019/08/16/hong-kongs-richest-man-appeals-to-anti-government-protestors--stop-the-violence/#239ad8575730

6) Protest activists are full time, pro-actively reaching out to foreign governments and foreign press

Many young protesters do not need to work as they are on strike and/or usually feed by their wealthy parents. Protesters are very organised with their own marketing team 文宣 and have another team focusing on contacting foreign governments and foreign press media to explain their views and seek supports.

Source: pro-protests social media

In contrast, older generations who are against the protests are going on work as usual. And there is also no point to contact foreign governments to express their support to China, isn't it?

7) Some have spoken out are mis-recognised as 'Chinese nationals' by the foreign press.

When I read TV news from Australia, I found that foreign press sometimes mistakenly labelled pro-Chinese Hong Kong locals as 'Chinese nationals'. Perhaps, some foreign press feels that those who support China must be Chinese nationals, not Hong Kong locals. (Though it is also true that quite a lot of people publicly speaking out for China in Hong Kong are indeed Chinese nationals or new immigrants from China to Hong Kong.)

Refer to Surprising Facts: 'How to differentiate if a source is from Hong Kong locals or from mainland China?'

8) Future belongs to the next generation

Some older generations do understand that the future belongs to younger generations. If the youngsters are dedicated to going against the government, it is the way they choose. Old people love their children and want to be loved, and are not as aggressive to confront the younger generations and break the relation.

Election of Chief Executive of Hong Kong – Controversies and Glory

One man, one vote?

The Chief Executive of Hong Kong is equivalent to a prime minister or a governor of Hong Kong.

Hong Kong community previously generally believed that 'one man, one vote' for the Chief Executive would be implemented in 2007/08 election. It was because the idea was supported by major political parties in Hong Kong.
https://zh.wikipedia.org/wiki/0708%E5%B9%B4%E9%9B%99
%E6%99%AE%E9%81%B8

Eventually, it did not happen in the 2007/08 election. But it had not sparked big protests. Perhaps, it was because Hong Kong people at that time were still quite happy about the society and did not really care how the Chief Executive is elected.

On 19-Sep-2019, Chief Executive CY Leung clarified that Sino-British Joint Declaration and the Basic Law had actually never promised 'one man, one vote' for the Chief Executive. If you read the two agreements, his claim appears valid.
http://www.2017.gov.hk/filemanager/template/tc/doc/second_round_doc/Consultation_Document_(Chapter_2)_Chi.pdf

Refer to: Surprising facts: 'Sino-British Joint Declaration/Hong Kong Basic Law'

When Hong Kong was a British colony:

It is worth to mention that Hong Kong citizens had never got 'one man, one vote' even in the time when Hong Kong was a British colony.

The governor of Hong Kong had always been appointed by the British. No one in Hong Kong could vote for his/her governor.

Also, the governor must be British.

Current system:

As mentioned earlier in this book, the Chief Executive (equivalent to a prime minister or a governor) has been elected by a local committee. When Hong Kong returned to China, this election committee only had 400 members. It was later expanded to 800 members and has increased to 1200 members since the year 2010. These 1200 committee members are elected by Hong Kong people.

In other words, currently, only the 1200 people who are elected by the people have the power to elect the Chief Executive of Hong Kong. Furthermore, it has been believed that some of these 1200 people's votes may be controlled by the Chinese government.

The Chief Executive must be a Hong Kong local, as specified in Sino-British Joint Declaration.

Controversies:

- In 2012 Hong Kong Chief Executive election, the three candidates were CY Leung, Henry Tang and Albert Ho. Hong Kong community generally feel that all three candidates are not the right people for the role.

Hong Kong people called CY Leung, '689', as he won with only 689 votes to rule Hong Kong's 7 million population.

- In 2017 Hong Kong Chief Executive election, candidate John Tsang was considered to be most loved by Hong Kong people. However, Carrie Lam won with twice his votes from the 1200-member committee.

It can be hard to understand why Carrie Lam insists many policies hated by the Hong Kong community and do not seem to benefit China. But it is also interesting that 'Firing Carrie Lam' was not one of the 5 demands by protesters.

The controversial extradition bill, 'Lantau Tomorrow Vision' and the destruction of the loved 'Lee Tung Street' (Wedding street) were all proposed or insisted by Carrie. Carrie claimed that the extradition bill was her own idea, not Chinese government's.

A positive example: Freedom of speech and freedom of protest. People won!

In 2003, Hong Kong people protested against the first Chief Executive, Tung Chee-hwa. Many complained Tung for his low-ability. The 2-time Chief Executive was soon fired by the Chinese government after those protests.

Unfortunately, I was also in that protest, but soon regretted. In later years, the Hong Kong community generally recognise Tung turned out to be the best Chief Executive in Hong Kong history to date.

Hong Kong, Before and after the Ex-British Colony became a part of China

Last 10 years of Hong Kong as a British Colony:

In the 1990s, Hong Kong biggest industries were financial services and tourism. Before 1997, many foreign tourists came to witness the disappearing British colony.

At that time, people are slightly wealthy and lives are affordable. Many families hire domestic helpers from the Philippines, Indonesia and Thailand. Families can usually afford to buy their own apartments, though a bit expensive.

Education had been compulsory for 9 years. Children learn English since they are 2 or 3 years old in Kindergarten. It was neither too easy nor too difficult to get to a university.

The governor of Hong Kong had always been appointed by the British. No one in Hong Kong could vote for his/her governor. Also, the governor must be British.

At that time, critics felt that the government/legislation departments were '議而不決, 決而不行' ('discuss but make no decision; decide but take no action'). However, at that time, the public was indifferent to politics. Hong Kong people were generally happy with their lives.

In terms of military, Hong Kong had been protected by Gurkha, who worked for the British Army.

1997: Just after Hong Kong returned to China

I was personally in Hong Kong before and after it returned to China.

There was not much obvious difference when Hong Kong just returned to China. One biggest difference was that tourists from foreign countries suddenly dropped significantly, as Hong Kong was no longer a 'disappearing British colony' and had become an ex-British colony.

1997 happened to be the year of the Asian financial crisis.

Custom between Hong Kong and China (such as its border in Shenzhen) was still very strict. Mainland Chinese could not easily get a permit to visit Hong Kong.

Military: Instead of Gurkha, China sends the People's Liberation Army to Hong Kong to protect the region (i.e. People's Liberation Army Hong Kong Garrison). But it was not noticeable to Hong Kong people, because soldiers and militaries have been rarely seen in the city in both British colony Hong Kong and Hong Kong SAR of China.

Tax: Tax rate in Hong Kong remained to be low and there were no major changes before and after Hong Kong returned to China. Salary tax is capped at 17%; or 15% of net income, whichever lower. There is no sales tax, no VAT, no GST. Only luxury items, such as alcohols and make-ups, are levied.

It is very different from mainland China, where individual income tax can be as high as 45%, with 13% VAT.

The Chief Executive (equivalent to a Governor) has always been elected by a Hong Kong local committee since Hong Kong returned to China.

Refer to Surprising Facts: 'Election of Chief Executive of Hong Kong – Controversies and Glory'

The first Chief Executive of Hong Kong, Tung Chee-hwa, had a slogan, 'Hong Kong strong, then China strong; China strong, then Hong Kong strong.'

10 years after Hong Kong returned to China, I interviewed a number of foreigners living in Hong Kong. Half of them were confused and thought Hong Kong was an independent country.

Since 1989 Tiananmen Square protests, many Hong Kong locals worried about what will happen to Hong Kong after it returns to China. Many migrated to overseas such as Canada, the United States, Australia and the United Kingdom. After 1997, Hong Kong looked all right. Many overseas' Hong Kong people returned to Hong Kong for settlement.

SAR outbreak

In the SARS outbreak in 2003, Hong Kong was one of the worst-hit cities in the world. After the outbreak, Hong Kong's economy was heavily impacted. Chief Executive of Hong Kong, Tung Chee-hwa, suggested opening Hong Kong's tourism to top-tier mainland cities like Beijing and Shanghai, in order to save the heavily tourist-dependent economy. In the beginning, it did help and Hong Kong people were happy.

So, Tung suggested opening Hong Kong's tourism to second-tier Chinese cities to boost Hong Kong's economy. Later, it was opened to almost all Chinese cities. Poorest people came to Hong Kong to only to buy necessities, crowding the streets and taking up public transports. It led to other problems, which will be discussed in the next section.

Problems in Hong Kong society before 2019 protests

Soaring Housing price:

Hong Kong apartments' price had risen by about 5 times, compared to just after SARS in 2004. With salary increase not that much, young couples are generally unable to afford to even get the loans for buying their own apartments.

Soaring housing price is believed to be caused by rich Chinese investors, the increased population of Hong Kong and insufficient land supply.

It is worth to mention that just before Hong Kong returned to China, housing price also used to be high (before the 1997 Asian financial crisis), but not as high as the present.

Refer to Supporting/References #7

Chinese immigrants to Hong Kong:

There are 3 main types of Chinese immigrants to Hong Kong:

1) Marriage visa holders

In the recent 30 years, many Hong Kong men marry women in China. Some complain that Hong Kong women are picky or materialistic – no matter if it is true or not, many decide to marry women from mainland China. There have been multiple confirmed cases that poor, old Hong Kong men living on social welfare can get young, beautiful wives from China. It is because people in China think Hong Kong people must be wealthy. Those Chinese wives only find that their Hong Kong husbands are broke when they arrive in Hong Kong after getting married.

Many of these Chinese wives are low-skilled and have low education levels. (How many rich, self-sufficient women would be willing to marry aboard to much older men?) Many live on social welfare after coming to Hong Kong. They are also given public housing, which most of the hard-working Hong Kong taxpayers are not eligible to apply for. Facing unaffordable housing, high living expenses and long working hours, many Hong Kong taxpayers decide not to have children. In contrast, jobless men and their Chinese wives give birth to children and can full-time look after children as their expenses are supported by social welfare.

This also leads to another problem: With a high volume of Hong Kong men marrying in China, many Hong Kong ladies remain single until the age of 40 or so. Single Hong Kong ladies need their own apartment, while Hong Kong men with their Chinese wives also need their own apartments. Housing demand doubled.

2) **Chinese parents give birth in Hong Kong. Children automatically become Hong Kong citizens by born.**

Both parents of these children had nothing to do to Hong Kong. But since they were born in Hong Kong, they automatically become Hong Kong citizens by born and enjoy all the social welfare, education and medical welfare that other Hong Kong citizens have. Theoretically, their Chinese parents can also become Hong Kong citizens, because of their Hong Kong children. They will then be entitled to the same welfare as the other Hong Kong citizens are, though they have never contributed to the economy of Hong Kong.

Hong Kong locals have been complaining about it. Unfairness in the allocation of social resources sparks anger in the Hong Kong community.

3) **Skilled immigrants**

Many countries attract skilled immigrants. But some Hong Kong locals complain that it is too easy to get skilled migration visa to Hong Kong from other countries such as India and China, threatening job opportunities of Hong Kong locals.

Nevertheless, the unemployment rate in Hong Kong has been very low, at least before 2019 protests.

https://www.macrotrends.net/countries/HKG/hong-kong/unemployment-rate

Accusation on over-priced contracts/infrastructures

Here are a few examples that Hong Kong locals accuse the government of paying for over-priced projects, wasting taxpayers' money. This book has no comment on whether these accusations are valid or not.

Source: multiple Hong Kong discussion groups & social media

- **Water supply**: Hong Kong does have its own reservoirs, but the supply was insufficient with its big population. Therefore, Hong Kong had long been relying on DongJiang water that Hong Kong government buy from China. In recent days, Hong Kong locals complain that DongJiang water is dirty and over-priced.
  Some argue that Hong Kong should implement seawater desalination. They argue that buying DongJiang water is for the benefit of China.

- **Hong Kong-Zhuhai-Macao Bridge**: as mentioned earlier in this book, many Hong Kong people feel that the construction of the bridge is too expensive and bring little benefits to Hong Kong.

- **'Lantau Tomorrow Vision'**: is a ridiculously expensive landfill project suggested by current Chief Executive of Hong Kong, Carrie Lam. This project will also vastly damage marine life in Hong Kong, destroy the livelihood of Hong Kong fishermen and kill eco-tourism of Hong Kong. Currently, Hong Kong still has dolphins and corals.
  https://www.bbc.com/zhongwen/trad/chinese-news-45886706

Inflation:

Minimum wage ordinance was introduced in Hong Kong in July 2010. Since then, there was obvious inflation in dining, especially in cheap, local restaurants.

Inflation in daily necessities was also caused by the high volume of Chinese tourists. Many go to Hong Kong to buy milk powders, shampoo and medicines, as goods in Hong Kong are considered to have guaranteed quality compared to mainland China.

Not many Hong Kong local manufacturing:

Hong Kong used to make high-quality clothes and watches. In recent 30 or more years, factories are moved to China for cheaper labours. Agriculture is also rare in Hong Kong due to the lack of land supply.

Food in Hong Kong is mainly imported from China. Rice, luxury items and high-class food are mainly imported from overseas.

Hong Kong is still a strong financial hub.

Why are Hong Kong people angry about the Hong Kong government and/or China before 2019 protests?

1. The rise of China

Before Hong Kong returned to China, Hong Kong used to be one of the top cities in the world, or at least in Asia. It has an unusual position as a rare British colony in the region, and it has been a strong financial hub. Asians such as Malaysians, Chinese, Singaporeans, Indonesians all love watching Hong Kong television series.

At that time, China was poor. Hong Kong people called mainland Chinese '阿燦', meaning they were old-fashioned and knew nothing about the big world. Relatives in mainland China loved to collect our old clothes as they still looked relatively new and high-quality. Illegal immigrants and illegal workers from China secretly travelled to Hong Kong because the wages in Hong Kong were far higher.

20 years after Hong Kong became a part of China, Hong Kong is still a strong financial hub, and still a top city in the world or at least in Asia. However, Chinese cities such as Shanghai, amongst the others, are also getting strong and wealthy. Many businesses go to China.

China has become wealthy. Now, mainland Chinese call Hong Kong people '港燦' (i.e. Hong Kong 阿燦), meaning they find Hong Kong people old-fashioned and know nothing about the big world. Relatives in mainland China now reject even new clothes my Hong Kong relatives donate. Rich Chinese enterprises take up some of the most expensive offices in Hong Kong.

Some Hong Kong people feel that these are the results of Hong Kong having been taken advantage of by China.

Refer to Surprising Facts: 'Problems in Hong Kong society before 2019 protests'

2. Lives are getting difficult in Hong Kong

Previously, Hong Kong people had long be regarded as indifferent towards politics. In the 2000s, you can often hear they say, 'We Hong Kong people are easy to please. We just want a good economy, happy lives and good living standards.'

In recent 20 years or so, lives in Hong Kong was getting difficult. Protest leaders suggested that difficult lives were the results of the lack of democracy.

These above two accusations may not be valid or may not be entirely valid. World changes. Under globalisation, developing countries has risen due to cheap labour, cheap costs, etc… In contrast, developed countries have been under the threat of soaring housing price, inflation, competition with offshore resources and factories moving to cheaper cities. These are not exactly Hong Kong specific problems.

Refer to Surprising Facts: 'Problems in Hong Kong society before 2019 protests'

3. Have always been worried, even before the handover of sovereignty.

Since 1989 Tiananmen Square protests, many Hong Kong people have always been worried about what will happen to Hong Kong after it returns to China.

4. A developed country governed by a developing country

Hong Kong has long been classified as a 'developed country' even before the Sino-British Joint Declaration was signed. (Although it has never actually been a country, it is undoubtedly, developed.) China has long been classified as a 'developing country' until today.

Many felt uneasy about being governed by a developing country.

5. Educated about the beauty of democracy, but under the rule of the communist

Being ruled by a democratic country, the United Kingdom, and have exposure to TV or books from the United States, Hong Kong people have long been educated about the good of democracy and the bad of communist.

Undoubtedly, democracy does have its beauty, but it has only become prevalent in the 20th century. Human beings had been under monarchies with no democracy before that.

6. Angry critics

In recent years, there had been many radio talk shows to criticize the government, namely programs by radio hosts Albert Cheng King-hon, Raymond Wong Yuk-man and Li Wei-ling. Their programs criticize the government, politicians or policies in Hong Kong, but the involved politicians or government departments would not be asked to respond. Everything they say is negative and in a very angry tone. You can barely hear they are appreciative in anything at all. You will surely be angry with the government and its policies after listening to their programs.

Defamation can occur. For example, radio host Li Wei-ling received a legal letter from Chief Executive CY Leung in accusation of defamation in 2018.

Nevertheless, these radio programs gain great popularity in Hong Kong. My relatives listen to these radio talk shows every day, believing they are 'smart' and 'loyal to the people' by their ability to point out the bad of the government and its policies. In later years, angry critics had become a kind of culture in Hong Kong. Pro-protests websites, protest leaders, pro-protests groups and even civilians supporting the protests get used to posting angry critics about the governments almost every day. Looking into Facebooks of my pro-protest ex-colleagues, almost every day they put on posts about the bad of the government and its policies. Their Facebook posts do not seem to have contents about themselves or about their own lives.

7. Press media

Since 2019 protests, pro-government civilians have called certain press media '黃媒 (yellow umbrella press media)', accusing them of biased news reporting to support the protests. Examples of alleged yellow umbrella press media include Apple Daily and Stand News.

On the other hand, pro-protest civilians have accused certain press media of pro-government news reporting. One example was television broadcasting company TVB, which was called 'CCTVB' as pro-protest civilians complain that it behaves like CCTV (China Central Television).

Jimmy Lai, the boss of Apple Daily 蘋果日報, was arrested under the new national security law in Aug-2020 and was soon released on bail. Apple Daily was founded by Jimmy Lai in 1995. It is worth to mention that Apple Daily has always been very popular but have never been reputable since day one.

According to a survey by the Chinese University of Hong Kong, the credibility of Apple Daily has been as low as pro-Chinese newspaper Wen Wei Po 文匯報 from 2001 to 2013.
http://www.com.cuhk.edu.hk/ccpos/b5/research/Credibility Survey%20Results_2016_CHI.pdf

Apple Daily has also long been considered immoral since day one. It is considered immoral in terms of how it competed in the market, its contents and how it reports news. For example, in 1998, Apple Daily had paid a notorious widower HKD 5000 to get prostitutes in China, for the sake of making news. Apple Daily had confessed paying him after he revealed it. Read more:
https://zhuanlan.zhihu.com/p/19624746

There are more than 30 newspapers, few radio stations and few television broadcasting companies in Hong Kong. Jimmy Lai of Apple Daily was the only one arrested under the new national security law, as of the time of writing.

https://en.wikipedia.org/wiki/List_of_newspapers_in_Hong_Kong
https://en.wikipedia.org/wiki/List_of_radio_stations_in_Hong_Kong

Sino-British Joint Declaration/Hong Kong Basic Law

Historic background:

In the 1800s, Chinese Qing government was very weak and lost a few wars. As a result, Qing government signed a few agreements to give or borrow different parts of Hong Kong to the British. In fact, many parts of China were given to the Europeans as a result of losing in wars.

Later, the new Communist Chinese government was established. They did not recognise the agreement that the old Qing government had signed with other countries. Also, these agreements were considered 'unfair'. Most lands given to European countries were later returned. Hong Kong was one of them.

What are the contents of the Sino-British Joint Declaration?

The Sino-British Joint Declaration was signed in 1985, between the United Kingdom and China over Hong Kong's sovereignty. In the agreement, Hong Kong's sovereignty would be returned to China from 1-July-1997.

Most important principles include 一國兩制 (One country, two systems), 港人治港 (Hong Kong people governed by Hong Kong locals), 高度自治 (High degree of autonomy) and 五十年不變 (50 years unchanged).

The details of the policy were written in the Hong Kong Basic Law. Hong Kong people would be governed under Hong Kong Basic Law from 01-July-1997, as a Special Administrative Region (SAR), as a part of China. Due to the clause '50 years unchanged'), such agreement should only last until 2047.

False hopes of the protests: Only 50 years unchanged

Protest leaders use the Sino-British Joint Declaration, 'One country, two systems', as a justification to fight for democracy only for Hong Kong, not for China. However, the Sino-British Joint Declaration will only last for 50 years, from 1997 to 2047. In other words, even if Hong Kong protesters successfully fight for all the democracy and the 5 key demands they request, these will only last for 27 years until 2047.

After 2047, Hong Kong will follow Communist China, as the Sino-British Joint Declaration will no longer be in effect.

How to differentiate if a source is from Hong Kong locals or from mainland China?

There have been accusations that mainland Chinese are pretending to be Hong Kong Chinese in the chaos. Here is how to differentiate them in terms of languages:

- **Different spoken language**: Cantonese is the official spoken language in Hong Kong; while Mandarin is the official spoken language in China. There are 300 spoken languages in China, but Mandarin was the official spoken language used by all people in China.

  Cantonese is well-agreed to be very hard to learn, much harder than Mandarin. Immigrants from China or other countries who join Hong Kong after the age of 10 almost always keep an interesting accent, differentiating them from local Hong Kong people. The accent will persist even after they stay in Hong Kong for another 70 years.

  It is worth to mention that Cantonese is also used in Canton China, i.e. Guangzhou, Macau, Zhong Shan, etc… But the Cantonese language of Hong Kong is slightly different from Cantonese languages of other parts of Canton China in terms of pronunciation and usage. Refer to the below.

- **Different written languages**: Traditional Chinese is the official written language in Hong Kong. Schools, newspapers, TV and local communities in Hong Kong all use Traditional Chinese.

Simplified Chinese is the official written language in China. Schools, newspapers and TV in China all use simplified Chinese.

- **Different terminologies**: Even if you use translators to translate the above different languages, they are still slightly different due to terminologies. One example is 'landlord' = '業主/业主'(traditional/simplified Chinese) in Hong Kong; while mainland Chinese call it '房東/房东' (traditional/simplified Chinese).

- **Different English accents**: In recent 30 years or so, native English-speaking teachers are introduced to Hong Kong. Therefore, younger Hong Kong locals can speak very fluent English, usually with an American accent.

  But for older Hong Kong locals, they were taught by non-native English-speaking Hong Kong teachers. Therefore, older Hong Kong locals' spoken English usually have an interesting accent. Native English speakers may not be able to understand them, while many older Hong Kong locals just do not dare to speak English in front of native speakers.

  As for mainland Chinese, not all can speak English. For those who can speak English, their accents are different from Hong Kong older generations'. Of course, some rich mainland Chinese can also speak fluent English if they studied in international schools or had studied aboard.

In conclusion, it is very easy for Hong Kong locals to differentiate Hong Kong locals from mainland Chinese, but it is not very easy for foreigners to differentiate them.

Another thing to look at: few newspapers are known to be pro-Chinese government, which I have avoided in this book. Other websites are known to be pro-protesters, which I only quote them if their words are showing their own faults. In principle, I try to avoid quoting all of them if possible.

The End

I hope you like this book. If you do, please write a review in Goodreads.com, Kobo, Amazon or other Internet book clubs.

Supporting/References

* 1. It is difficult to get an exact figure on the ratio of local Hong Kong citizens supporting vs against the protest. It is because statistics from either side or from whatever organization are likely to be biased. However, within the Hong Kong community, it is generally believed that the ratio is 50% to 50%. While some argued it might be 60% to 40% in the later stages of the protests, apparently, the majority still believe the ratio is 50% to 50%.

Source: multiple Hong Kong discussion groups & social media

In later part of the book, we have quoted the survey from The Chinese University of Hong Kong and the University of Hong Kong regarding Hong Kong people's opposition rate against the extradition bill which sparked the protest. However, opposing the bill does not necessarily mean supporting the protests.

* 2. It is publicly agreed that the best three universities in Hong Kong are: The University of Hong Kong, The Hong Kong University of Science and Technology and The Chinese University of Hong Kong. The 4th and 5th are City University of Hong Kong and The Hong Kong Polytechnic University. The 6th best university is Hong Kong Baptist University. Lingnan University that Nathan Law and Yau Wai-ching graduated from to is publicly agreed as the 7th best university (i.e. second-worst) in Hong Kong. The Open University of Hong Kong that Joshua Wong graduated from was only granted university status in May 1997, now the 8th best university (i.e. the worst) in Hong Kong.

You can see the same in Wiki, as of the time of writing Jul-20.

* 3. I cannot find the statistics on the exact number of bachelor's degree holders in Hong Kong. However, according to newspaper SCMP, almost one in two young people in Hong Kong go to university:

https://www.scmp.com/comment/insight-opinion/article/1856458/university-degree-hong-kong-no-longer-worth-what-it-once-was

Education in Hong Kong is free. Primary education and junior secondary education (a total of 9 years) are compulsory. https://en.wikipedia.org/wiki/Education_in_Hong_Kong

* 4. Protesters translate '光復香港' as 'Liberate Hong Kong'. However, literately, '光' = 'shine, '復' = resurrect'. Therefore, literately, '光復' has nothing to do to 'Liberate'.

* 5. Dual universal suffrage is not a main topic of this book. This book gives you a brief idea. If you are interested in this topic, you can research more.

* 6. Protest activists had declared multiple times that the protest/unrest would continue if any one of the 5 key demands is not met: https://www.youtube.com/watch?v=2XbuPvN2rUQ

* 7. Hong Kong housing prices had always been known to be very high. Below is one of the references dated 31-May-2019, just before 2019 Hong Kong protests:

https://www.hk01.com/%E5%9C%B0%E7%94%A2%E6%A8%93%E5%B8%82/335436/%E6%A8%93%E5%83%B9%E6%96%B0%E9%AB%98-%E6%A8%93%E5%83%B9%E7%99%B2%E5%8D%87%E8%83%8C%E5%BE%8C-3%E5%A4%A7%E7%8F%BE%E8%B1%A1%E4%BC%BC%E8%B6%B31997%E4%BA%9E%E6%B4%B2%E9%87%91%E8%9E%8D%E9%A2%A8%E6%9A%B4%E5%89%8D

It says '樓價持續攀升下，終再創歷史新高。中原城市領先指數（CCL）報 189.42 點，超越去年 8 月時的 188.64，是歷史以來最高。CCL 於 1997 年 7 月時僅為 100 點，2003 年沙士期

間更跌至 31 點的低位，即現在的樓價已較 1997 年樓市狂潮時高出 80%，更是沙士時樓價的 5 倍有多。' ('Hong Kong housing prices are in a historic high. Housing Price Index CCL in July-1997 <*when Hong Kong just returned to China, before 1997 Asian financial crisis* > was 100 points, CCL was lowest at 31 points in SARS, and now <*before Hong Kong 2019 protests*> it is 189.42 points.')

* 8. According to statistics, Hong Kong's retail location is the most expensive in the world as of June 2019: https://www.statista.com/statistics/264903/most-expensive-shopping-streets-for-retail-rent-worlwide/

The position must have changed after the 2019-20 Hong Kong unrest and COVID19 in 2020.

www.ingramcontent.com/pod-product-compliance
Lightning Source LLC
Chambersburg PA
CBHW062151020426
42334CB00020B/2556